DEION SANDERS

MR. PRIME TIME

BY BILL GUTMAN

MILLBROOK SPORTS WORLD
THE MILLBROOK PRESS
BROOKFIELD, CONNECTICUT

Library of Congress Cataloging-in-Publication Data
Gutman, Bill.
Deion Sanders: Mr. Prime Time / Bill Gutman.
p.   cm.—(Millbrook sports world)
Includes bibliographical references and index.
ISBN 0-7613-0224-7 (lib. bdg.)
1. Sanders, Deion—Juvenile literature. 2. Football players—United
States—Biography—Juvenile literature. 3. Baseball players—
United States—Biography—Juvenile literature.   I. Title. II. Series.
GV939.G186G87   1997
796.332'092—dc21
[B]   97-5644 CIP   AC

Photographs courtesy of © Paul Spinelli/NFL Photos: Cover; Allsport:
Cover inset (© 1995 Al Bello), pp. 39 (Otto Greule), 42 (Jonathan
Daniel); AP/Wide World: pp. 3, 7, 12, 19, 20, 23, 28, 37, 46; Focus
on Sports: pp. 4, 21, 25, 35, 44; © Florida State/NFL Photos: p. 14;
© Ryals Lee/Florida State/NFL Photos: p. 16; UPI/Corbis-Bettmann:
p. 27, 30, 32.

Published by The Millbrook Press, Inc.
2 Old New Milford Road
Brookfield, Connecticut 06804

DEION SANDERS

On October 16, 1994, the Atlanta Falcons met the San Francisco 49ers in a battle for first place in the National Football Conference Western Division. It was an important game, and one that had a special meaning for the Niners' All-Pro cornerback, Deion Sanders.

Deion had spent his first five years in the National Football League with the Falcons. During that time, he had built a reputation as the best cornerback in the league at covering a pass receiver one-on-one. But that wasn't the only special thing about Deion Sanders.

He had become an All-Pro football star while also playing major-league baseball. And he had succeeded at both as only Bo Jackson had done before him. So when he joined the 49ers for the 1994 football season, Deion was already

NFL wide receivers dread the imposing sight of Deion Sanders playing across the line of scrimmage. No matter what uniform Deion has worn, he has remained the best cornerback at covering receivers in the open field.

considered one of the great all-around athletes of his time. He was also one of the showiest.

With the nickname "Prime Time," Deion loved to perform on the gridiron stage. He strutted and high-stepped on the field. Off the field he drove flashy cars and wore gold chains and diamond-studded jewelry. He cut a rap album and was often seen mugging for the camera. Some called him the perfect example of the self-promoting, ego-driven athlete.

But Deion's critics forget that it takes hard work and total dedication to play two major sports with hardly a break and become the best at your position. Deion couldn't have done that if he was only concerned about being a showman and promoting himself.

That October afternoon against the Falcons was typical Deion Sanders. Atlanta had one of the best wide receivers in the business, a gamebreaker named Andre Rison. Deion would be going up against Rison, head to head. These were the kinds of challenges Prime Time loved the most. The best against the best.

As a cornerback, Deion was very fast and explosively quick. He could stop and start, change direction, and shift into high gear in an instant. He was one of the few cornerbacks who could make a mistake and recover quickly enough to make a great play. And every time he got his hands on the football, there was a good chance that he would take it all the way to the end zone.

But that wasn't all. Deion also liked to play mind games with his opponents. That's what he did with Rison. Early in the game the two superstars tangled after a play and got into a brief fight. It was all Deion needed.

"After that, Andre's entire game just went out the window," said Falcon assistant coach Milt Jackson. "Deion did what he wanted to do, which was to get into Andre's head, and Andre didn't play well at all. In that game, Deion controlled at least one quarter of the field."

In a key October 1994 game against the Atlanta Falcons, Deion ran an interception back 93 yards for a San Francisco touchdown. The Falcons had been Deion's first NFL team, but that day he helped defeat them, 42–3, to keep the Niners in first place.

Deion covered Rison closely on every play. The three catches Rison made were all for short yardage and didn't hurt the Niners at all. And in the second quarter, Deion picked off an Atlanta pass at the San Francisco 7-yard line. He started up field, using the moves of a halfback and a speed second to none. A couple of key blocks by his teammates helped out, and he was gone, returning the pass 93 yards for a San Francisco touchdown. As always, he high-stepped the final 5 yards into the end zone and then did a hotdogging victory dance. Again, it was Deion's way.

Deion sat out most of the second half with a pulled muscle. Yet he had done the job. When the game ended, the 49ers had a 42–3 victory. Rison finished with just five catches for 32 yards, and just three of those had come against Deion. In addition, Deion's 93-yard touchdown return was the second longest in team history.

The man called Prime Time had been doing that kind of thing since he was eight years old. He was always a star, a guy whose desire to excel in sports may have saved his life. And to the surprise of many, the flamboyant rap-singing athlete that the public sees is a different kind of person when he's out of the bright lights.

A DANGEROUS CHILDHOOD

Sports has always been one way for a youngster to stay physically fit, learn discipline, and be a team player. In some cases sports provides a way to keep kids off the streets and out of trouble. Sometimes, however, the love of sports can literally save a life. Such was the case with Deion Luwynn Sanders.

Deion was born on August 9, 1967, in Fort Myers, Florida. His parents, Connie and Mims Sanders, lived in a very poor section of the city. His mother was a hardworking woman, who sometimes held two jobs. There was a time when his father did some work with mentally retarded children. But by the time Deion was born, Mims Sanders was caught up in the drug world that was all around them.

Shortly after Deion was born, Mr. Sanders left the family and remained a habitual drug user for many years. As Deion would say later, "He wasn't there with me, but he was just around the corner."

Unfortunately, there were drugs around the corner as well. In fact, they were everywhere, a threatening trap for almost every young boy and girl growing up there. Luckily for Deion, he had a strong mother and also the intelligence to see what was happening.

"My mother broke her back working in a hospital cleaning rooms, but she always had time to teach me right from wrong," he said. "And I knew early on that my father did drugs. I saw what that stuff could do, so why would I want to be like him?"

But as he grew older, there were temptations. One by one, many of his early childhood friends drifted into drugs, both using and selling. Young Deion knew they were making mistakes that would cost them dearly later on. And if he had had nothing to do but hang out, Deion might have joined his friends and given in to the temptation of drugs. But early on, he had discovered something else: sports.

"Ever since I began playing sports I was always the best one on the team," he said. "I was always the man, even at eight years old. Because of that, I never had to fit in with the wrong crowd."

That was the truth. Deion had speed and skill from the start. When he was just 9, he was already outrunning and generally outplaying 14- and 15-year-olds. Everyone wanted him on their team. By the time he was 12 he was a celebrity in his neighborhood.

And he did it without smoking, drinking, or doing drugs. Even his friends felt he would become a big baseball, football, or basketball star and make millions of dollars.

Deion admits that getting rich was always one of his goals, even if he wasn't always poor as a child. Some years after his father left, Connie Sanders became Connie Knight. Deion got along very well with his stepfather, and because both his mother and stepfather worked, the family's quality of life improved.

"I've always had things," he said, looking back at his teenage years. "I was always well-dressed, had jewelry, and had a car when I turned 16. Plus my family always stuck together."

Deion played Little League baseball and countless hours of other sports in the parks and in the streets around Fort Myers. As he got older, he continued to excel at sports, while his friends continued to fall victim to drugs and crime.

"I'd say to them, 'Have you ever seen a drug dealer retire?'" Deion remembered. "They couldn't answer that one. They knew I was right, but they kept at it. Now maybe 70 or 80 percent of my childhood friends are doing time in jail. And a few of them are no longer here."

By the time Deion arrived at North Fort Myers High School in the fall of 1982, he was ready to show people just how good he had become. So far he had avoided the dangers of drugs and crime thanks to sports and a strong family. Now he was ready to take the next step.

ON TO FLORIDA STATE

At North Fort Myers High School, Deion went about becoming a star. He found time for baseball, basketball, and football. He was always coachable and anxious to learn. Even then, Deion didn't take sports lightly. He had a world of natural ability, but wanted more.

Deion was a well-rounded student-athlete at North Fort Myers. He kept his grades up, became involved in activities such as ROTC, and continued to improve as an athlete. By the time he was a senior, he had become the outstanding athlete many always felt he would be.

On the football team he was a left-handed option quarterback, as well as the team's best defensive back. During his senior year, he passed for 839 yards and rushed for another 499. The numbers would have been even better if he hadn't been set back by a knee injury the second half of the season. When the season ended, he was an All-State selection.

He was also All-State in both basketball and baseball. He averaged 24 points a game on the hardwood and hit well over .300 on the diamond. He was an exciting performer in all three sports. His speed was dazzling and often brought the crowds to their feet. A number of colleges were already pursuing him, including big-time rival schools, such as the University of Florida, the University of Miami, and Florida State University.

Deion decided to attend Florida State University in Tallahassee, Florida. The Seminoles, under Coach Bobby Bowden, had one of the top college football programs in the country. There were many outstanding young players coming to Tallahassee. In the fall of 1985, Deion Sanders quickly proved to be one of them.

Although Deion went to Florida State with the idea of becoming a wide receiver, he quickly saw there were too many wideouts ahead of him on the depth chart. So he changed his priorities and switched to defensive back.

"I didn't want to sit on the sidelines," he said, "and I knew if I was a wide receiver, I had little chance of playing."

So he became a cornerback and a punt returner. He also came prepared. That summer he worked out with FSU's outstanding wide receiver Hassan Jones. That gave Deion the confidence that he could become a good cover man on passes.

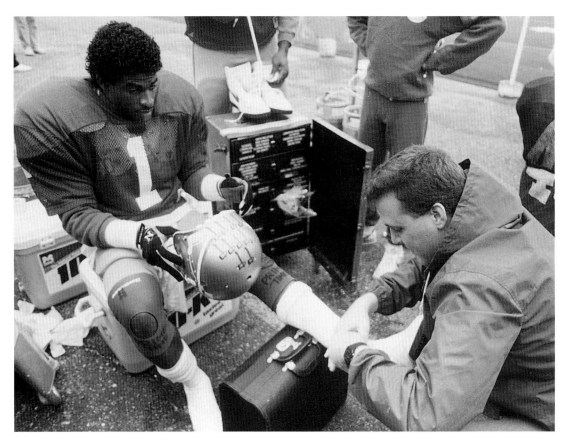

A young Deion has his ankles taped before a practice session at Florida State. Deion's nickname, "Prime Time," can be seen written on his knee supports.

"I was confident I could play the pass as soon as fall practice began," Deion said. "The run has been tougher. I have trouble getting the blockers off me and getting to the ball carrier."

Although Deion didn't start in the first three games of the season, he played cornerback in spots and returned punts. The third game was against Memphis State. The Seminoles had a 16–10 lead with five minutes left, but Memphis

State had the ball. They were a touchdown and an extra point away from winning. Regular right cornerback Eric Williams was bothered by a sprained ankle, and suddenly Deion was in the game at crunch time.

Memphis State had a fine wide receiver in Jerry Harris, who had played an outstanding game against the Seminoles the year before. With the untested Deion in, Coach Bowden was worried.

"I saw the matchup and I was going crazy," was the way the coach put it.

Memphis State quarterback Danny Sparkman tried to exploit the freshman immediately. But when he passed the ball to Harris, Deion was there to deny the Tigers a completion. Florida State hung on to win.

"Sanders had him covered like a blanket," Coach Bowden said.

"I was nervous at cornerback in the first two games," Deion said, assessing the situation, "but I'm pretty comfortable now. I still haven't learned how to play the run well, but I'm getting better."

He went on to have a fine freshman year, starting three games, and seeing considerable action in all the others. In a big game with Florida, he took a punt back 58 yards for a touchdown. Against Tulsa, he intercepted his only pass of the year. But with his usual flair for the dramatic, he returned the pickoff 100 yards for a touchdown and a school record.

When the regular season ended, the Seminoles had an 8–3 record and were ranked in the top 20. Deion finished with 42 tackles, 4 pass deflections, and an interception. He also returned 30 punts for a total of 255 yards, an average of 8.5 yards per return. Now FSU had to meet Oklahoma State in the Gator Bowl. And once again Deion Sanders picked a big game to show his talents.

As the Seminoles rolled to a 34–23 victory, Deion made six tackles, broke up a big pass, and picked off another. The win gave the Seminoles a 9–3 record and a national ranking of 15th in the final Associated Press poll.

Deion was a superior all-around athlete at Florida State. His sweet swing at the plate and speed on the bases and in the outfield resulted in his being drafted by the New York Yankees.

But Deion didn't rest on his laurels. That spring, he went out for the base-ball team and played half a season until an ankle injury put him on the shelf. He still managed to hit .333 with 11 stolen bases and 14 runs batted in in 16 games. It seemed that to excel in one sport just wasn't enough.

PRIME TIME ALL-AMERICAN

In his sophomore year of 1986, Deion really began to stand out. He already had the nickname Prime Time, which had been given to him by a good friend in high school. In fact, many of his friends simply called him "Prime" or "Time."

The Seminoles had a winning football season, but were not a top 20 team. Deion started 9 of 11 regular-season games. He had 61 tackles, sixth best on the team. He led FSU with 4 interceptions, caused 2 fumbles, and had 8 pass break-ups. He also returned 31 punts for 290 yards, an average of 9.4 yards per return.

After the season, the Seminoles went to the now defunct All-American Bowl and defeated Indiana, 27–13. Then Deion learned he had been named his team's defensive Most Valuable Player. In addition, he was named a first team defensive back on the *Sporting News* All-American team. The Associated Press named him a third team All-American, while the United Press named him to its honorable mention squad.

But perhaps the greatest athletic feat of Deion's sophomore year came during the spring of 1987. Deion was part of the baseball team again, and had also joined the track-and-field team. He had trouble at the plate all season, hitting just .221, but still managed to dazzle with his speed, stealing 28 bases. Then came the Metro Conference baseball tournament, and Deion did something that became legendary around the Florida State campus.

During the tournament, the Seminoles had two games in one day. That same day, a track meet was being held. Deion played in the first game. As soon as it was over, he rushed to the track and ran a leg on the 4 x 100 relay team—in his baseball pants! It was his first track experience, and Deion's team won the race. He then raced back to the diamond to play the second baseball game and wound up smacking the game-winning hit. As amazing as it sounds, Deion was just doing what came naturally. His talent and athletic ability apparently knew no bounds.

Deion (left) surprised a lot of people at Florida State when he joined the track team and began recording world class times in the 100-meter dash. He even helped the track team win a relay race between the games of a baseball doubleheader.

When Deion's junior year of 1987 rolled around, he was once again set to take center stage on the gridiron. With the Seminoles in the running for the national championship, Deion played brilliantly all year long. He became only the sixth consensus All-American in school history, being named first team on every major poll. FSU finished the season with a 10–1 record, third in the nation and right behind unbeaten Miami, the only team to defeat the Seminoles.

In the postseason Fiesta Bowl, the Seminoles defeated fifth-ranked Nebraska, 31–28, and were ranked second in the nation behind Miami.

That year Deion had picked off another four passes and broke the school record with 381 punt return yards. He brought one kick back for a touchdown and made several other spectacular returns. What couldn't be found in the statistics was the fact that he had also shut down several outstanding wide receivers. A number of people were already calling him the best college cornerback in the country.

Then, during the spring, he made the surprising decision not to play baseball, but to focus instead on the track team. Again, the results were astonishing. In just his third 100-meter race, he sprinted the distance in 10.26 seconds—a world-class time that qualified him for the NCAA championships and also for the Olympic trials that were to be held that summer.

But Prime Time still wasn't finished. He won the 100- and 200-meter dashes at the Metro Conference Championships and then joined teammates Sammie Smith, Dexter Carter (both future NFL players), and world-class hurdler Arthur Blake to win the 4 x 400 meter relay.

The 1988 Summer Olympics would be held in Seoul, South Korea, but Deion wasn't interested because the Games would take time away from football, and he wasn't about to jeopardize his football career. Whether Deion would have made the Olympic team will never be known.

His busy life wasn't about to slow down. Despite not playing baseball in the spring of 1988, Deion found himself drafted by the New York Yankees, which took him in the 18th round. He surprised a lot of people by signing a contract with the Yanks, telling team officials he wanted to return to Florida State for his senior year.

The Yankees agreed. That summer, Deion played in the low minors, making stops at Sarasota and Ft. Lauderdale, Florida, before getting a three-game look at Columbus, the Yankees' Triple-A farm team. He proved to be a speedy outfielder with a world of potential. When he returned to FSU in the fall of 1988, he indicated that he wanted to continue his professional baseball career. It was beginning to look as if Deion Sanders might be good enough to play two professional sports.

PRIME TIME TAKES CENTER STAGE

Deion loved the attention that came his way during his last year of college. He was a preseason All-America choice once again and quickly lived up to his reputation as an outstanding cornerback.

By now, opposing quarterbacks tended to throw the ball away from Deion's side of the field. And when they did throw in his direction, he was always ready. He picked off five more passes as the Seminoles were again among the top teams in the country, losing only to archrival Miami. He took two of his five interceptions back for touchdowns, averaging 23.2 yards a return.

In addition, he led the nation with a 15.2 average on punt returns. And he closed out his college career by helping the Seminoles to a 13–7 victory over Auburn in the Sugar Bowl. FSU finished at 11–1 and was ranked third in the nation.

Once again Deion was a consensus All-American at cornerback, and after the season was named the winner of the Jim Thorpe Award as the best defensive back in the country. Everyone who watched him now knew him as Prime Time, a complete showman on the football field. But he was also a player who backed up his actions with his deeds. Even then Deion said that Prime Time was only his football personality.

With his flair for the dramatic, Deion closed out his college football career with a game-saving interception in the Sugar Bowl. His pickoff enabled Florida State to defeat Auburn, 13–7.

"When the lights go on, it's Prime Time for me," he said. "It's like Jekyll and Hyde. It's two different personalities. When I have to put on a show I put on a show. But when I'm out with my friends, I'm a mellow kind of guy. I don't even listen to fast music."

But the public would rarely see that part of Deion, and many had the wrong impression of him. Nevertheless, Deion knew that his Prime Time personality could be a great marketing tool. It could help him earn a lot of money.

During the summer of 1989, Deion again played baseball in the Yankees organization. He also learned that he was the number-one draft choice of the Atlanta Falcons of the National Football League, and was the fifth player taken—that's how good the NFL people felt he was. But he held off signing with the Falcons so he could concentrate on baseball.

A jubilant Deion raises his arms after learning that he was the number-one draft choice of the Atlanta Falcons. He was the fifth player taken in the entire draft.

He had a good year. He played well enough in the minors to earn a midseason promotion to the Yankees. Deion was just one year out of Florida State, and he was already in the big leagues.

Deion played just 14 games for the Yanks in 1989, batting .234. He also had the chance to play center field at spacious Yankee Stadium, the same turf once patrolled by all-time greats Joe DiMaggio and Mickey Mantle. But it was still too early to tell if he had the goods to be a real baseball superstar.

On September 5, Deion belted his second big-league homer for the Yanks. Two days later, he signed a contract with the Atlanta Falcons and reported immediately. His NFL debut came on September 10, against the Los Angeles Rams. The Rams won the game, 31–21, but that didn't stop Deion Sanders from showing the football world that he belonged.

Midway through the game Deion fielded a Rams punt on his own 32-yard line. He avoided the first wave of tacklers with

When Deion returns a punt, there is a good chance that he will go all the way. He has tricky moves and blazing speed, making him hard to stop in the open field.

some sharp moves, then cut quickly to the sideline and turned on the speed. Not surprisingly, no one could catch him. He pranced into the end zone for a 68-yard touchdown return. It was a remarkable debut. And it also made him the only athlete in history to hit a major-league home run and score an NFL touchdown in the same week.

Though the Falcons were just a 3–13 team in 1989, Deion excelled. He finished the year with 5 pass interceptions, and ran back 28 punts for 307 yards, an 11.0 average. He also took back 35 kickoffs 726 yards, a 20.7 average per return.

People had already begun to wonder whether Deion would pick one sport over the other. He said his intention was to play baseball in the spring and summer until it was nearly time for football. Then he would report to the Falcons and play the entire NFL season.

STAR TO SUPERSTAR

In the eyes of most people, Deion had always been a better football player than a baseball player, and this still appeared to be the case in the pros. He perceived the two games very differently.

"Football is straight-out ability," he said. "Football is physical—strength and instinct. Baseball is mental, because the sport sets you up for failure. Plus, if I score a touchdown or intercept a pass, I can enjoy that all week. In baseball, you hit a home run and that's it. The next night, the next at bat, you're starting over. You can't master baseball. You can just learn more about it."

What Deion meant is that with 162 games to a baseball season, a hero today can be a goat tomorrow. There are just 16 games to a football season. A player has a whole week to savor a victory, a great runback, or a key interception. It certainly sounded as if he favored the gridiron game.

The next couple of years seemed to bear that out. He batted a scant .158 in 57 games when the Yankees called him up in 1990. After the 1990 season, the

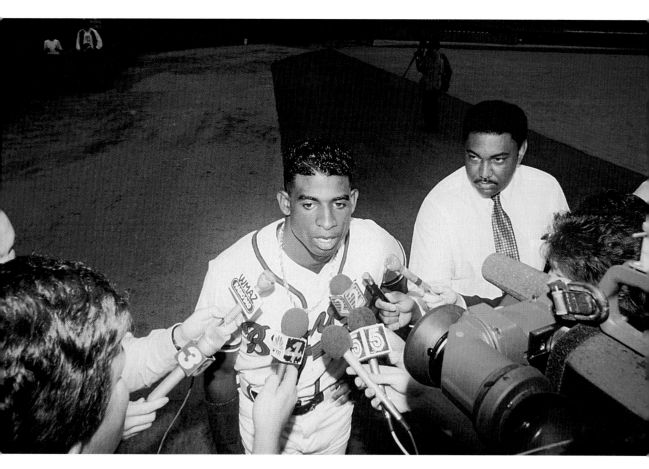

Glad to be here. Deion greets the media after joining the Atlanta Braves for the 1991 season. Now he would be playing both baseball and football on the same field.

New Yorkers seemed to give up on him, allowing him to sign with the Atlanta Braves. Next year, he would be playing both sports in Atlanta.

The 1990 football season was a different story. He started all 16 games for the Falcons, playing cornerback and returning kicks. Not surprisingly, his play was spectacular. His 82-yard interception return for a touchdown against the Houston Oilers was the longest touchdown play in the entire league that year.

Later, he set a Falcons record by returning a punt 79 yards for a score against the Bengals. And against the Dallas Cowboys, he had a 61-yard return of an interception for another touchdown that clinched an Atlanta upset victory.

The 1991 seasons were very similar. With the Braves, Deion bounced back and forth between the majors and minors and batted just .191 in 54 games. Unless he began hitting better, Deion knew that his baseball career might be short-lived.

As usual, football seemed to be his priority. In 1991, Deion was voted a starter in the postseason Pro Bowl game. He was also NFL Defensive Player of the Week on two occasions. The Falcons surprised everybody by finishing at 10–6 and making the playoffs as a wild-card team. They then beat the New Orleans Saints before losing to the Washington Redskins in the Divisional Playoffs.

It was hard to see how Deion could continue playing baseball with his football career in high gear. But in the spring of 1992, things changed. Deion was hitting well during spring training and opened the season as the Braves center fielder. After 13 games, he was batting .426 with a league-leading six triples. Batting coach Clarence Jones helped Deion change his stance so, as a left-handed batter, he could hit left-handed pitchers better. It was all working.

"I've got to where I know in my heart I'm going to go out there and get two base hits every day," Deion said. "That's my goal."

Deion looked like a coming star at the outset of the 1992 baseball season. After just 13 games, his smooth left-handed swing had produced a .426 batting average and a league-leading 6 triples.

Hitting coach Jones said Deion's success was the result of hard work.

"Before, he would just grab his bat and go up there and hit," the coach said. "Now he prepares himself before every game: who's pitching, what they're throwing, and how they're trying to get him out. Now, he's using his head along with ability."

The Braves had one of the best teams in baseball and had an excellent chance to reach the World Series. But by August, Deion was in a mild slump and nearly down to .300. Otis Nixon was now the Braves' everyday center fielder with Deion platooning in left with Ron Gant. Deion had to decide whether to leave the team for football, or stay through the playoffs.

He knew that the Falcons needed him more than the Braves. But for the first time he was having real success with baseball. He didn't know what to do.

"I want it all, all," he said. "But you can't have it all in this world. So I need to make a decision. I need to know my destiny. I want the zoo to stop. The best thing is, I know either way I'm going to win, even though either way I'm going to be giving something up."

At this point, Deion wasn't making the so-called big bucks. The Braves were paying him $600,000 to play through July 31 (the date he was to report to football training camp), and $125,000 for each month he stayed beyond that. The Falcons were paying him a base salary of $750,000 per year. He was reportedly negotiating with both teams for long-term contracts. Each still wanted him to guarantee them a full season.

Once again, Deion did the unusual. He began dividing his time. He stayed with the Braves, but practiced with the Falcons on off days. He knew he would miss the first few games of the football season. The Falcons would have to live with that.

When the regular baseball season ended, the Braves were National League Western Division champions with a 98–64 record. Deion had had his best sea-

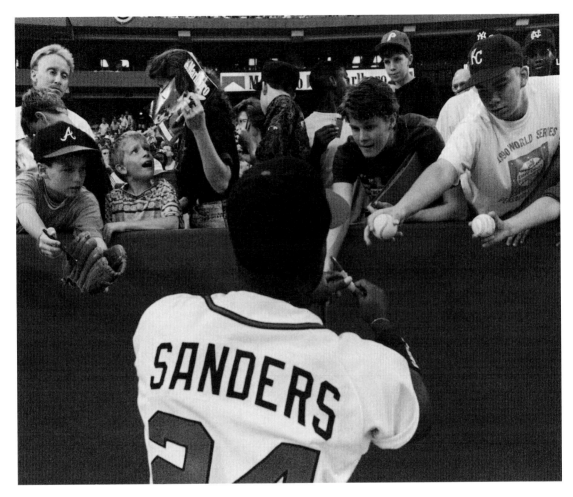

The 1992 season was Deion's best as a baseball player. He hit .303 for the Braves and helped them into the World Series, where he batted .533. He was also popular with the kids who came to see "Prime Time" play.

son yet. Limited to 97 games by injuries and being platooned, he still hit .303 with 6 doubles, 14 triples, 8 homers, and 28 runs batted in. He also stole 26 bases. In the National League Championship Series, the Braves would have to meet the Pittsburgh Pirates.

After four games, Atlanta had a 3–1 lead. Game 5 was to be played on Sunday night, October 11, at Pittsburgh. That Saturday, Deion made a surprise announcement. He said he would jet to Miami that night to play in the Falcons-Dolphins game the next afternoon, then jet back to Pittsburgh for the Braves-Pirates game Sunday night. He would become the first professional athlete ever to play two sports in one day.

In his usual Prime Time style, Deion pulled it off. He did a fine job for the Falcons, then saw some action in the baseball game, which the Pirates won, 7–1. However, he soon found himself criticized. Some said he did it for the publicity,

When Deion played for the Falcons against the Dolphins in Miami, then took a helicopter to Pittsburgh to join the Braves in a battle against the Pirates on October 11, 1992, he was the first person to play in two professional sporting events in one day.

that he went back on his word to stay with the Braves until their season ended. One writer said he had a huge ego that was out of control. Later, Deion gave his version of the story.

"The story should have been that I was breaking my neck to help both of my teams," he said. "I don't need publicity. I wasn't being selfish and didn't have an attitude. I just wanted to help my teams."

The Braves won the playoffs in seven games. But Deion had just five at bats. He failed to get a hit and struck out three times. Those who said he had burned himself out by playing both sports, however, would have to eat their words. For Deion was about to have a great World Series against the Toronto Blue Jays.

The Braves and the Blue Jays split the first two games, with Deion going 1-for-3 in the second game. In game three, he had three hits, including a double, though the Braves lost, 3–2, in ten innings. He sat out the fourth game, which the Blue Jays also won, then had two hits and an RBI in game five, which Atlanta won, 7–2. Finally, in game six, he had two more hits and a run scored, but Toronto won it in ten innings, 4–3, to capture the 1992 World Series in six games.

All told, Deion led both clubs in hitting, batting .533 with 8 hits in 15 at bats. He also showed his great speed with five stolen bases. For the first time in his big-league career, Deion looked like a real star. His only disappointment was that the Braves lost.

After the World Series, he immediately reported to the Falcons and became the NFL leader in Pro Bowl balloting at both cornerback and kick returner. He led the NFL in kickoff returns, with an average of 26.7 yards a return. While he had only three pass interceptions, it was because quarterbacks now tended to throw away from Deion's side of the field. But with his success in the World Series, there were new questions about what he would do. Would he choose one sport over the other?

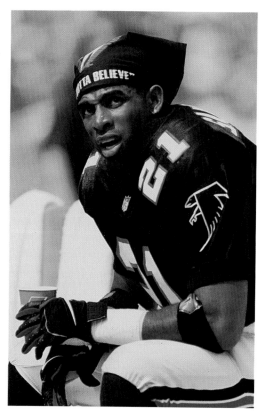

Although he was playing baseball during the week and football on the weekends during the early part of the 1992 NFL season, Deion was still spectacular. Here he catches his breath on the Falcons' bench after running a kickoff back 99 yards for a touchdown against the Washington Redskins.

DEFENSIVE PLAYER OF THE YEAR

The next two years were a mixed bag for Deion. Things continued to go well on the gridiron. Baseball, however, remained far more unsettled. After his success in the 1992 World Series, his agent began negotiating a new contract for him. It looked like it would be his first multimillion-dollar pact.

But the deal was not yet done when the 1993 season began. Deion was again a part-time player, and there was something else happening in his life. On April 23, Mims Sanders died of a brain tumor at age 50. Deion left the Braves to attend his father's funeral. He and his father had become much closer in recent years. Deion had even gotten him a job with rap singer M. C. Hammer.

After the funeral, Deion didn't return to the Braves for nearly three weeks. Finally, in early May, the team placed him on the disqualified list, claiming that Deion refused to return because he didn't have a new contract. Once again he was called selfish. Deion felt that he was being punished for not signing the contract that the team had offered.

When he did return to the Braves, he signed a three-year contract in the $11 million range. But many of his teammates, he said, were more interested in his contract than the fact that he had lost his father.

"I'm bitter because it was the first time I'd lost someone close to me, first time I'd ever been to a funeral," Deion said. "All everyone cared about was the Braves. I was thinking about my father dying, and my mind was nowhere near baseball. That's why I left. I was starting to go crazy."

Some say it was never the same between Deion and the Braves after that. He wound up the 1993 season hitting .276 in 95 games. Then, because his contract called for him to finish the baseball season, he played in just 11 games for the Falcons. Even so, he led the NFC with seven interceptions and was named NFC Defensive Player of the Month for November. He was also the only NFL player in 1993 to rush the football and catch a pass from scrimmage on offense, intercept a pass on defense, and return punts and kickoffs. In fact, he caught six passes for 106 yards, an average of 17.7 yards a catch. And that included a 70-yard touchdown reception. Once again he was voted a starter in the Pro Bowl.

Although committed to baseball, Deion was obviously a more solid performer in football. And it was on the gridiron that he paid special tribute to his father. He always wore a wristband printed with "MS," his father's initials.

"After my father died I would take him out there on the field with me," Deion said. "I would go up to the line, get ready to cover somebody and look over my shoulder and say, 'You all right over there? You OK, Pops?' I worked my butt off. I dedicated the season to my father and had a good year.

"And every time I get a base hit [in baseball] or make a big play in football, you'll see me tap my chest twice and point to the sky. I'm pointing to my father."

Deion's baseball career seemed to unravel more in 1994. He was hitting a solid .288 for the Braves in June and playing almost every day when he was abruptly traded to the Cincinnati Reds for center fielder Roberto Kelly.

"I'm here to play ball and win games," Deion said. "I was surprised to be traded, but now I'm looking forward to the change."

He played hard for Cincinnati, hitting .277 in another 46 games. He ended the season with a career best 38 steals, but had only 4 homers and 28 runs batted in in 375 at bats with both teams. He was an exciting baseball player, but far from a great one.

Nothing can take away Deion's enthusiasm for playing sports. Despite a surprise trade from the Braves to the Cincinnati Reds in June of 1994, Deion stayed upbeat. Here he greets the media with Reds' team owner Marge Schott and General Manager Tim Bowden.

Things also changed that year in football. With his contract up, he became a free agent. Atlanta had fallen to 6–10 in 1993, and Deion wanted to be with a team that had a chance to win the Super Bowl. He surprised a lot of people by signing a one-year pact with the San Francisco 49ers for $1.1 million. He would earn another $750,000 if the team won the Super Bowl. That's what Deion wanted.

The Niners had won four Super Bowls in the 1980s and were again a superior team. They had finished at 14–2 in 1993, but had lost, for the second straight year, to the Dallas Cowboys in the NFC title game. The team hoped the addition of Deion would help put it back on top.

Veteran 49er center Bart Oates saw Deion's impact after just a few games.

"I can compare him to [former Giants linebacker] Lawrence Taylor," said Oates. "Everybody played better when Lawrence was there. I saw the same thing happen when Deion came. The front guys played better. The linebackers tended to play together. For whatever reason, he is able to elevate the performance of his teammates."

Once again, he was a one-man highlight film, producing great plays almost every week. Because of baseball, he joined the team late and got his first start against the Saints on September 25. Deion made 8 tackles and took back an interception 74 yards for a score. He was promptly named NFC Defensive Player of the Week. That set the tone for his season.

The Niners finished the 1994 regular season with a league best 13–3 record. Deion finished with six interceptions, but he brought three of them back for touchdowns. More and more offenses were staying away from him. In fact, in the divisional playoff game against the Bears, the Chicago quarterback didn't attempt a single pass in his direction. San Francisco won the game, 44–15. Deion's greatness was recognized when he was named the NFL Defensive Player of the Year.

WINNING A PAIR OF RINGS

Now it was time to try to help his teammates get to the Super Bowl. The first hurdle was the NFC title game with the Cowboys. Dallas had stopped the Niners here the past two years. But this was San Francisco's day. The Niners took a 21–0 lead after just 7 minutes, scoring after 3 Dallas turnovers.

The 49ers won it, 38–28, as Deion successfully defended five passes and made a big interception at the San Francisco five-yard line to stop a Dallas drive. Next came the Super Bowl. The 49ers would be going up against the AFC champions, the San Diego Chargers.

Once again the Niners made it look easy. With quarterback Steve Young throwing a record six touchdown passes, the Niners won easily, 49–26. It was the fifth championship for the 49ers, but the first for Deion Sanders. As expected, he played a brilliant game. He had four tackles, stuck to pass receivers like glue, and picked off a Stan Humphries pass.

"This is truly my dream," Deion said. "I could taste it. This is a great team. They would have made the playoffs without me. I was brought here for this one game. And, we prevailed."

Though quarterback Young got most of the praise for his fantastic passing day, Deion did his usual work. One writer called his play against Dallas wide receiver Alvin Harper "pure genius." After six years in the league, his work at cornerback was admired by everyone.

After joining the San Francisco 49ers in 1994, Deion continued to play at an All-Pro level. Here he breaks up a pass intended for the Dallas Cowboys' Alvin Harper (80). The Niners won the Super Bowl that season, and Deion wound up as the NFL Defensive Player of the Year.

"He takes one-third to one-half of the field away from the offense," said wide receiver Flipper Anderson.

"When we played him in '94," said Saints star receiver Michael Haynes, "we talked about not even bothering to throw his way. It was part of our game plan to keep the ball away from him. He can take away that much."

But Deion wasn't doing it on natural ability alone. He worked hard and long to improve his play against the run and to know the receivers he'd be covering.

"It's instinct and it's knowing the game," he said. "People think I don't study because I make it look easy. People think I don't know the guys, and don't know game situations. I know situations. I watch that guy come out of the huddle. I pretty much have a grasp of what he is going to do before the ball is snapped based on the situation and the distance. I know the game of football."

Deion was more popular than ever. He was getting more endorsement deals that sent his off-field income soaring. He was marketing the Prime Time image that many people resented. Prime Time often came off as cocky and arrogant. To Deion, though, it was simply a way to earn money.

"I knew a long time ago that quarterbacks make a lot of money, running backs make a lot of money, but defensive backs don't make a lot of money. I created Prime Time so I could build my mother her dream house and make sure she never has to work a day in her life."

Deion was also a committed family man who spent as much time as he could with his wife, Carolyn, and two children, Deion, Jr., and Diondra. It hurt him when he had to miss his daughter's first T-ball game.

"I don't care what they say about me when I'm through with sports," he explained. "I don't want to be known as anything else in life but a great father."

After helping the 49ers win the Super Bowl, many thought Deion would finally leave baseball and concentrate on football. He was again a free agent and could sign with any team, commanding a huge contract. But by April he was back in action for the Cincinnati Reds.

It didn't go well. On May 31, he severely sprained his left ankle while sliding into third base, and was out for 6 weeks. Then, shortly after his return, he found himself traded to the San Francisco Giants. Deion finished the season with the Giants, hitting .285 in 52 games. He had hit just .240 with the Reds in 33 games. It was apparent that time was running out if he expected to be a baseball superstar.

But Deion had created big news even before the end of the baseball season. There was a bidding war for his services between the 49ers and their archrival, the Dallas Cowboys. On September 9, 1995, it was an-

Traded to the San Francisco Giants in 1995, Deion still gave his all to the game of baseball. But more people began to believe that he would give up baseball to concentrate on football.

nounced that Deion had signed a mammoth 7-year contract with the Cowboys. It was said to be worth some $35 million, including a $13 million signing bonus.

"I'm glad it's over," Deion said, after signing. "Every man owes it to his family to get security."

Once the baseball season ended, Deion learned he needed arthroscopic surgery to repair his injured ankle. He didn't play a game for the Cowboys until

October 29, but quickly picked up his first interception in a 28–13 win over his former team, the Falcons.

The Cowboys were a powerful team, featuring Troy Aikman, Emmitt Smith, and Michael Irvin on offense. They had won two Super Bowls before the Niners had derailed them in 1994. Now, with Deion at cornerback, they hoped to get the championship back.

Pretty soon, Deion was up to his old tricks, playing close to the best cornerback in the league. His new teammates quickly saw the kind of guy he was off the field, too.

"There are things people don't know about Deion because it doesn't get publicized," said offensive lineman Nate Newton. "He doesn't drink. He doesn't do drugs. He doesn't cuss. He's a strong family man. He's only flashy when he's out in the public entertaining."

Sure enough, Deion picked another winning team. The Cowboys won their division with a 12–4 record. Then they opened the playoffs with a 30–11 victory over the Eagles. In that game, Deion lined up at the wide receiver position, took the ball on a reverse, and ran 21 yards for a touchdown.

"I've never seen anything like it," said quarterback Troy Aikman. "It was absolutely unbelievable."

Then, in the NFC title game, the Cowboys whipped the Green Bay Packers, 38–28. Besides playing his usual game at cornerback, Deion also caught a 35-yard touchdown pass from Aikman. He was doing it on both sides of the ball,

With the Dallas Cowboys in 1995, Deion often played both offense and defense. In the Super Bowl against the Pittsburgh Steelers, Deion played cornerback, and as a wide receiver caught a 47-yard pass from Troy Aikman to set up a Dallas touchdown.

playing both offense and defense. Now the Cowboys were back in the Super Bowl, this time facing the Pittsburgh Steelers.

Again it was a tough game. And once more Deion performed on both defense and offense. In the second period, he caught a 47-yard pass from Aikman that set up a Dallas touchdown and a 10–0 lead. Later in the period, he made a defensive gem, knocking away a long pass intended for Pittsburgh receiver Yancey Thigpen. After that, the Steelers stayed away from Deion's side of the field. That gave the other Dallas cornerback, Larry Brown, the chance to pick off a pair of passes as the Cowboys won, 27–17.

Deion now had two straight Super Bowl wins with two different teams. And in both cases, many felt he was the difference. Once again, he had been true to his word and got the job done.

TWO-WAY SUPERSTAR

The huge contract from the Cowboys had given Deion the security he wanted. Now he just wanted to be the best football player he could be. So he didn't play baseball in 1996.

During the off-season he began building a dream house near Atlanta and kept busy with many commercial endeavors. He also spoke to groups of youngsters about the dangers of drugs.

"I tell kids if drugs and alcohol were good for you, you'd have your lunch and a joint for dessert," he said. "But you don't because it's not good for you. It's wrong. . . . Just about everything bad is alcohol- or drug-related."

At the outset of the 1996 football season, the Cowboys learned they wouldn't have star wide receiver Michael Irvin for the first five games. Deion volunteered to start at both cornerback and wide receiver.

Deion trained extremely hard to be in condition to play both positions. He was still considered by most a superb defensive back. Former coach and current television commentator John Madden put it this way: "Deion is the first player to be able to dominate and dictate a game from the defensive back position."

But when the 1996 season started, Deion was playing both ways. In the Cowboys' opening-game loss to the Chicago Bears, he was on the field for an incredible 107 plays. Although the Cowboys struggled in the early going, people still marveled at Deion's skill and stamina.

Even when Irvin returned, Deion continued to start on both offense and defense. In game 10, the Cowboys took a 20–17 overtime thriller from the 49ers. Deion caught two passes for 34 yards and did his usual solid job at cornerback. The team was now 6–4 and back in the running for a divisional title.

When it ended, Dallas had a 10–6 record to win the division. Despite some minor injuries, Deion finished with 36 catches for 475 yards and a touchdown as a wide receiver. On defense, the opposing team didn't throw his way very often, so he intercepted just two passes. But he was still an All-Pro.

Unfortunately, it wouldn't be another Super Bowl year for the Cowboys. The team opened the playoffs with an easy 40–15 victory over Minnesota. But in the NFC Divisional game, they were upset by the Carolina Panthers, 26–17. In the fourth quarter Deion left with a concussion and fracture of the right eye socket. But he had played his heart out once more.

Shortly after the season ended, Deion surprised everyone. He announced that he was returning to baseball. He signed a one-year deal with his former team, the Cincinnati Reds.

"I'm a natural football player," he said. "But something has to present a challenge, and this is my challenge. I always have to challenge myself."

The Reds were happy to have Deion back. General Manager Tim Bowden knew Deion was motivated to return.

"He really wanted to succeed in two sports," Bowden said. "Football is easy to him. In baseball, he has a lot to prove."

So Deion set about proving it. He was again playing centerfield and leading off. And while the Reds were not a winning team, Deion began having the best season of his baseball life. By the third week in June he was hitting .319 with 88 hits in 276 at bats. He had three homers and 17 RBIs. But more importantly he was sixth in league hits, tied for the most triples with 6, and he was leading the league with 31 stolen bases. For the first time, he was playing like a real all-star.

It has truly been an amazing career for the man known as Prime Time. He has been a World Series winner and a Super Bowl champion. No one else has ever played two professional sports in one day.

Deion never seems to want to slow down. Yet when asked what he is going to do when he retires, he just smiles and says:

"Fish, fish, fish. I'll just fish all day. It's straight-out therapy for me. So when I retire I'll fish and take my kids to school to make sure they get a proper education."

But when he is performing for huge crowds, Deion is still Mr. Prime Time. According to him, that will never change.

"It's always been my dream to light up the stage," he has said. "I want to do everything I can for my team, even if that means never coming off the field."

In 1996, Deion was called upon for his offensive and defensive skills nearly full-time. Here he catches a Troy Aikman pass in the season opener against the Chicago Bears, beating defensive back Walt Harris (27).

DEION SANDERS: HIGHLIGHTS

1967   Born on August 9 in Fort Myers, Florida.

1985   Enters Florida State University.
Returns intercepted pass for a school record 100 yards and a touchdown.

1987   Becomes consensus All-American as defensive back.

1988   Wins Metro Conference championship in both the 100- and 200-meter dashes.
Drafted by the New York Yankees to play baseball.
Becomes consensus All-American in football a second time.
Wins Jim Thorpe Award as best college defensive back in the country.

1989   Plays baseball in Yankees organization.
Was number-one draft choice of the Atlanta Falcons of the NFL.

1991   Signs with the Atlanta Braves to play baseball.

1992   Plays NFL football game and major-league baseball game on same day (October 11).
Hits .533 in World Series for the Braves.
Voted starter in NFL Pro Bowl.

1994   Traded to Cincinnati Reds in baseball.
Joins San Francisco 49ers in football.
Helps 49ers win Super Bowl championship.
Named NFL Defensive Player of the Year.

1995   Traded to San Francisco Giants in baseball.
Signs with Dallas Cowboys in football.
Helps Cowboys win Super Bowl championship.

1996   Announces retirement from baseball.
Plays both defensive back and wide receiver for Cowboys, becoming a rare two-way player.
Named first team All-NFL at cornerback.

1997   Ends baseball retirement by signing with Cincinnati Reds.

FIND OUT MORE

Chadwick, Bruce. *Deion Sanders*. New York: Chelsea House, 1996.

Gutman, Bill. *Football*. North Bellmore, NY: Marshall Cavendish, 1990.

Harvey, Miles. *Deion Sanders: Prime Time*. New York: Children's Press, 1996.

Savage, Jeff. *Deion Sanders: Star Athlete*. Springfield, NJ: Enslow Publishers, 1996.

Weber, Bruce. *Pro Football Megastars*. New York: Scholastic, 1994.

How to write to Deion Sanders:
Deion Sanders
c/o Dallas Cowboys
One Cowboys Parkway
Irving, TX 75063

INDEX